How to Make a Card

written by
Karen Evans & Kathleen Urmston

Title: How to Make a Card
Copyright © 2014 Kaeden Corporation
Authors: Karen Evans & Kathleen Urmston

ISBN: 978-1-61181-511-5

Published by:
    Kaeden Corporation
    P. O. Box 16190
    Rocky River, Ohio 44116
    1-(800)-890-READ(7323)
    www.kaeden.com

Printed in Guangzhou, China
NOR/0614/CA21400856

First edition 1995
Second edition 2002
Third edition 2007
Fourth edition 2014

Table of Contents

Supplies

You will need pink paper, red paper, scissors, glue, glitter, **lace**, ribbon, a pencil and an **envelope**.

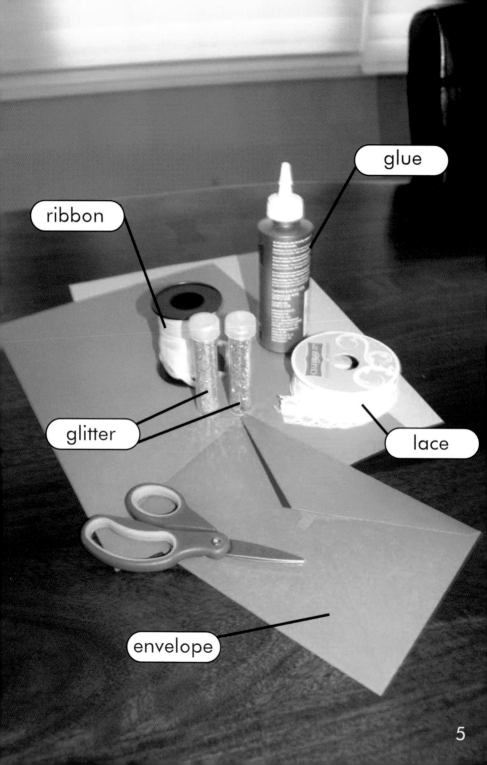

glue

ribbon

glitter

lace

envelope

5

The Message

Fold the pink paper in **half**. Open the paper and write a **message** inside.

Decorating

Cut out a red heart.

pencil line

folded side

scissors

To make a symmetrical heart, fold your paper in half and draw a half of a heart on the folded side.

9

Glue the red heart
on the pink paper.

Glue some lace on the heart.

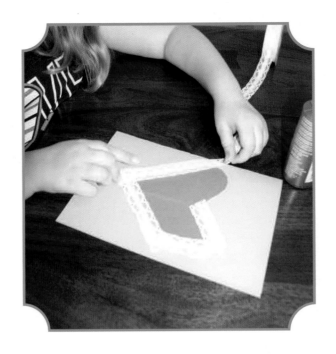

To get the lace in the shape of a heart, it is helpful to cut the lace into smaller pieces.

Write with the glue and **sprinkle** on some glitter.

When finished, carefully shake the excess glitter off into a garbage can.

15

Put the card in the envelope. Make a bow and glue it on the envelope.

Allow the glue to dry before putting it into the envelope.

bow

The Delivery

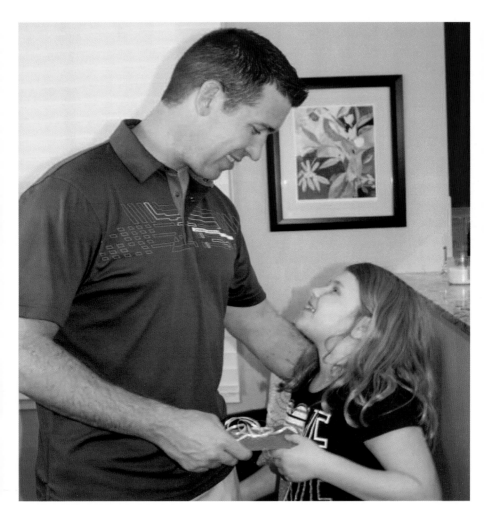

Give it to someone special!

Glossary

envelope - a flat paper container for a letter or thin package, usually having a flap that can be sealed

half - one of two equal parts

lace - a delicate decorative fabric that is woven in a symmetrical pattern

message - a communication sent from one person to another containing information

sprinkle - to scatter or distribute in drops

Index